The Marrow's Telling:
Words in Motion

Also by Eli Clare:

Exile and Pride:
Disability, Queerness, and Liberation (1999)

The Marrow's Telling:
Words in Motion

Eli Clare

Homofactus Press
Ypsilanti, Michigan

Published in 2007
by Homofactus Press, L.L.C.
www.homofactuspress.com

The following reprinted with permission:
"And Yet": *Self Organizing Men*
"Angels": *Anthology of Magazine Verse and Yearbook of
    American Poetry; Hanging Loose*
"Battle Rock": *Cultural Activisms: Poetic Voices, Political Voices*
"Bedrock": *Sinister Wisdom*
"Cleaning Dead Birds": *Lesbian Ethics*
"Clothes," "Scars," and "Stone": *From the Inside Out: Radical
    Gender Transformation, FTM and Beyond*
"East Oakland": *The Arc of Love*
"Escape": Dangerous Families: *Queer Writing on Abuse*
"In the City": *The Women's Review of Books*
"Gawking, Gaping, Staring": *GLQ: Desiring Disability; Queer
    Crips: Disabled Gay Men and Their Stories*
"How to Talk to a New Lover About Cerebral Palsy": *Cultural
    Activisms: Poetic Voices, Political Voices; My Lover Is a
    Woman: Contemporary Lesbian Love Poems; Staring
    Back: The Disability Experience from the Inside Out; The
    Arc of Love*
"Interludes I–VI": *Out in the Mountains*
"Learning To Speak": *Poetry from Sojourner: A Feminist
    Anthology; Sojourner: The Women's Forum; Staring
    Back: The Disability Experience from the Inside Out*
"Left with the Ocean": *Evergreen Chronicles*
"The Stories Mama Tells": *The Disability Rag*
"The Terrorist God": *Sinister Wisdom*
"To the Curious People Who Ask, 'What Do Your Tremors Feel
    Like?'": *Michigan Review; Points of Contact: Disability, Art, and
    Culture*
"Tremors": *My Lover Is a Woman: Contemporary Lesbian Love
    Poems*
"Words and Breath": *Agenda; Evergreen Chronicles*

Printed in the United States of America
Some rights reserved.
ISBN:978-0978597313

Table of Contents

The * marks pieces that include details about child sexual abuse, torture, and/or ritual abuse. See note on page 7.

Acknowledgements

Without community this book would simply not exist. For companionship, support, encouragement, and many hours of conversation over the years, a big thank you to Alison Bechdel, Jessica Colinares, Diana Courvant, Susan Cowling, David Dierauer, Patricia Fontaine, Amber Hollibaugh, Joanna Kadi, Alison Kafer, Deirdre Kelly, Riva Lehrer, Harriett Lewis, Samuel Lurie, Annette Marcus, Sebastian Margaret, Adrianne Neff, Claire Neff, Heba Nimr, Sarah Paige, Suzanne Pharr, Mary Frances Platt, Tovah Redwood, Jay Sennett, Skip Shewell, Scott Solik, Eli Trudeau, and Ethan Young.

I wouldn't be half the poet I am today without a number of teachers and writing buddies. Bill Beckman, Jan Clausen, Kenny Fries, Jewelle Gomez, Joanna Kadi, Sarra Lev, Nora Mitchell, and Su Penn all had a hand—directly or indirectly—in shaping the pieces in this book.

With brilliance, humor, and patience, Joanna Kadi edited this book in its various incarnations over the last 15 years. Jay Sennett and Gwyn Hulswit of Homofactus Press stepped forward as publishers extraordinaire and brought it to life. My partner Samuel Lurie jokes that he became a manuscript widower as I worked long focused hours at the computer, recited stanzas in the shower, and simply stopped doing my fair share of housework. Nonetheless he stuck it out, for which I am more than grateful.

And finally I want to acknowledge two activists, who, although they never read these poems and prose pieces, greatly impacted this book and my work in general.

Alexander John Goodrum (1960–2002): African–American, transgender, queer, and disabled, Alexander and I had long conversations about disability and trans identities and how ableism and transphobia intersect. His gentleness and compassion always brought me back to the importance of honoring lived experience, whether it meshed with my politics or not. He killed himself while under suicide watch at a psychiatric hospital. His life strengthened me, and his death haunts me.

Heather MacAllister (1968–2007): White, queer, femme, fat and anti–racist activist, founder of Big Burlesque: The Original Fat Bottom Revue, Heather impacted my thinking about bodily difference in profound ways. Eight months before her death of ovarian cancer, she spoke to a gathering of fat dykes, bisexual women, trans folks, and allies at NOLOSE's annual conference. She said:

> We can talk about fat liberation until we're blue in the face, but if we don't love our bodies, we will never have it.... Our oppression is sited on our bodies; our bodies are the direct target of hatred. So true healing has to include a physical component, and it is ongoing since fat hatred is ongoing. I want to make a distinction between 'positive body image' as a personal growth phenomenon and fat activism as a radical social movement. They do not have to be separate. In fact, each can only succeed with the other.... Surround yourself with fat–positive images. Stop reading *Cosmo* and

watching TV. Get naked in front of a full–length mirror. Get a tattoo on the fattest part of your body and show it off. Touch, tattoo, decorate, reveal, show off the fat parts of your body. Have sex naked, with the lights on. Swim naked. Eat mindfully and gratefully. Move. Sweat. Wear comfortable clothing—lose the girdle....*

Heather left such a mark with her commitment to body love and pride as forms of resistance.
Alexander and Heather, here's to you, wherever you are now.

— Eli Clare
May 2007

---

* For the full text of Heather's speech, see
http://www.nolose.org/06/hm_keynote.php

Author's Note

The pieces listed here are in part about child sexual abuse, ritual abuse, and/or torture and include graphic, but not gratuitous, details. As such, they may contain triggers. Please take as much care as you need.

"Cleaning Dead Birds"
"Last Refrain"
"No Longer Small and Lonely"
"Psych Ward in Three Voices"
"Bedrock"
"Escape"
"Stone"

Also note that I've changed a few names and identifying details to protect my privacy and the privacy of others.

"Our bodies are nobody's occupied territory." —
Ibrahim Farajajè

DEDICATION

To Samuel, Joanna, and Sebastian
for your sustenance of many kinds—I can't possibly
conjure words enough.

Echoes: A Preface

I grew up in a narrow valley, the river and a single expansive hayfield squeezed between steep hills. My siblings and I spent many an hour at the gravel bar, abandoned apple orchard, and milk barn. We were allowed to wander as far as our mother's voice could reach. Before supper, she'd step out the back door and send a holler rolling through the valley.

I started work on *The Marrow's Telling* knowing that history and identity send echoes through our bodies. The reverberations bounce around inside us, sometimes fading into silence, but often lingering, amplified in the body's bellows and chambers. I set out to explore the chaos of these echoes. I pulled poems and prose pieces from two decades of writing, seeking not coherence but complexity. I remembered how a valley carries a morning–time holler in one way, an evening–time holler in another; how summer air cradles sound differently from winter air.

In the United States, too many of us have been taught to fear or avoid poetry, to feel bored or stupid in its presence. As an activist–poet, I want this book to be a door held wide open. Read it like a demonstration, a riot, a late night spray–painting action.

Laying poem next to poem, I invited contradiction as well as repetition. In the process of revision, I made myself a deal. I could strengthen the language but not change the story. The poem written 15 years ago about the first Gulf War couldn't morph into being about the current war in Iraq. The story about coming out as a dyke in the backwoods of Oregon had to keep its shape, even though I live today as a genderqueer, a white guy on the streets, not yearning back toward dyke identity but unwilling to abandon that part of who I've been. I wanted this book to gather and weigh the echoes in the same ways our bodies do.

> Don't start at the beginning nor finish at the end. Read this book as if it were a rollercoaster, a parachute opening above you, a slow meandering river.

We rarely heard her voice but rather its echoes bouncing back. We'd leave whatever we were doing, our initial reluctance overcome by a desire for food and dry clothes. Race up the hill, hay in our hair, mud smeared on our pants, tracing the echoes back to their source.

> Don't worry about chronology; at the bottom of each piece, I've left a track, a date, a reference point.

The stories in the following pieces range from the damage reeked by Christian missionaries to a retelling of my birth, from child sexual abuse* to disability politics. They emerge from no one source but many intimate history, community knowledge, activist thinking, letters of a long–ago white explorer and the sweep of my imagination today, all intertwined, all somehow connected to the body.

Let the six "Interludes" be pauses, exhortations for each of us to tell a tangle of stories, to translate them across chasms and listen hard in our home communities. Allow your own breath to be a single thread wending its way through these pages.

In the end, I stand at the crossroads where private and political, public and personal meet, but I don't want to stand here alone. And so, please, join me in chasing echoes down to the marrow, tracing their sources back to a lover's hand, a bully's taunt, a wild blue sky.

written 2007

---

* See author's note on page 7.

Thin Silver Notes

The one who wears language
warm against her breastbone:

> Which dreams are memory,
> rhythm of leg and lung
> and heart mile after mile?

The drowning one who hauls
his own heavy self back to land:

> Which poems are flesh and which
> are dream: did we dance the day
> Nelson Mandela went free?

The one who carries a rifle, swings a crowbar,
walks through shards as her neighborhood burns:

> Which memories will be forgotten,
> only to return: dream of flood, dream
> of fire, dream of children torn loose?

The one who comes close
to thin silver notes of death:

> Which poems refuse to lie and which
> lies tell a truth: fierce and rough, whatever the
> terror, shake this into memory.

after the riots in los angeles 1992
written 1992

Learning to Speak

Three years old, I didn't talk,
created my own sign language,
didn't walk but stumped
all over the house on my knees
growing thick calluses.
Words slow dance
off my tongue, never leap
full of grace. They hear
blank faces, loud simple replies.
I practiced the sounds *th, sh, sl*
for years, a pianist playing endless
hours of scales. I had to memorize
the muscle of my tongue.

childhood 1966
written 1992

Vow

Rain all day, almost snow,
remaining leaves rattle
in the wind, cornfields mowed
to stub. Onion and lentils
simmering, I stir a bay leaf
into the pot, crumple
another into my hand.
                    That smell:
Oregon summer, and I'm halfway
up the hill to my house,
wind and river hush,
myrtle fills the air.

Crumpling leaf into hand
as if to repeat a vow.

remembering Oregon 1990
written 1991

Angels

Late afternoons as shadows
overtake the valley, I lay myself
in the riffle where stream
meets river, water warmed all day
and still cold, current pulls, finger bones
tremble. I hang onto rocky bottom
long as I can, then give way,
body rushing downstream
to steadier water. Dive deep
to swim along the green
gold river bed, salmon
nibble, lungs strain. And finally
after the sun has disappeared,
hills leaning closer, I leave
the clasp of angels, return
to weight of bone and muscle.

Elk River 1979
written 1991

Abandoned Firetower

Wave upon wave the hills
roll away—axis, fulcrum,
horizon. We ride
the updraft: no smoke,
no thunder, no smack
of lightning, just the blue
scoop of sky, wind rocking us
five stories high.

Later, descending back
to earth, only later
do I remember. The long-legged
leap of flame tree to tree
twenty years ago. South-central
L.A., Detroit, Philadelphia burning
still. The house fire my brother once flung
himself from. Gravity pulls hard
to sun-baked granite.

green mountains 1992
written 1995

Interlude I: Tug

Our deepest stories depend upon so much: language, music, history, food, spirit, romance, sex, the very marrow itself. We find these stories through connection, whether with family or community, trees and rocks, or sidewalks and subway trains, the quiet or clamor inside our heads. They form bedrock; they shift over time; they pull across the grain. And all too often we try to tell them in single, lone words

In trans community, we're in the midst of creating a myriad of words: transgender, femmeboy, ftm, transwoman, transsexual, genderqueer, trannyboi, mtf, crossdresser, transman, transie, two spirit, femme queen. *Some we've adopted from doctors and sexologists, others we've found in dictionaries or stolen from the bullies and bashers, and still others we've created ourselves.*

These lone words can be useful but never enough: Eight–years–old, I carried my kite down to the hay-fields and sheep pastures, flew it for hours on end, spinning line out, five hundred feet, a thousand. I can still feel that tug on my arm.

written 2005–2007

Old Country Endearment

Mama rocked me to sleep
with an old country endearment,

last fragments of a language
she didn't speak and Grandma

abandoned to the streets of Detroit.
And great Grandma, the cornfields

never spoke English. I search
the dictionary for that one word. River

at dusk, I'd throw my baseball cap
high, watch the bats circle it down

again and again nearly to the gravel bar,
then veer away, flickering in dim light.

Mama's voice, *Ja Lieschen*, I circle it down,
but the dictionary pronounces *Liebchen*.

I veer away, consonants shift: an old country
endearment no longer a real word.

childhood 1968
written 1991

Cleaning Dead Birds

I.

My father's students brought him
gunny sacks of dead birds—ducks
and geese they had shot
at Garrison Lake. They lumbered up
to our house, rifles stashed in trucks,
rubber boots muddy, mumbled
about hunting season, too many birds
that afternoon, see you Monday
Mr. Johnson, left quickly.

We cleaned the mallards
at his workbench, shop soon
smelling of wet feathers
and burlap, he cut their gizzards open,
showed me the dark grit inside.
I played with the guts, blood
on my hands and shirt.

Eating the roasted birds,
sometimes I bit down
on buckshot.

II.

My father plans
his second wedding,
traces the old maps —
foot of Humbug Mountain,
Sixes River Grange Hall,
church on 6th Street.

The girl soon to be his stepdaughter:
will she walk the logging roads
with him, learning the shape
of rocks and forest, books
and music, only to wear
his semen nearly
transparent against her body
as I once did.

Spend hours in the woodshop
watching as he sands and oils
bird's eye maple, then together,
cleaning dead birds.
Fear tastes like buckshot.

III.

After the vows
my father stands
outside the Grange Hall,
beard trimmed tight. He drinks
champagne, smiles, poses.

The danger too real:
whether they clean
dead birds together
or not, laugh wildly
after dinner, or become
family sure as salmon
run upriver to the spawning
beds every year,
he must stop here.

I warn my stepmother,
tell her the stories
he denies, pitting
memory against memory,
proof lodged in my body.

childhood 1971, wedding 1991
written 1991

Whale Bone and Ash

Forty-one sperm whales, long
as logging trucks, beached
themselves on South Jetty when
I was fourteen. They blew
warm streams of air from
their blow holes, whoosh
and sigh, every five minutes.

People lined up for miles, took Polaroid
pictures, pried teeth from bone, carved
initials and swastikas into living flesh.
Boys hopped whale to whale as if
they were driftwood logs until
police barricaded the beach.

Not the death of animals
sheltered deep inside a briar patch,
but public: I wanted to caress
their obsidian sides, pour handfuls
of salt water over them,
lay my body down on the sand.
First blood stained my thighs,
floated and sank in clots. My mother
celebrated, but I wanted the privacy
of climbing trees, skipping
stones, wading knee-deep
in the river. Bones ached, body
learning to clench.

The whales stopped breathing
slowly, lungs collapsing under
earth-bound weight. They pounded
the beach with their flukes, died
mewing in the rain. Later a crew
arrived with chainsaws and bulldozers,

idled and roared through
blubber and bone, blood joined
tide. They burned what they could,
all-night bonfires, gasoline-soaked
pyres, buried the rest, pink
ribbons decorated the sand.
That summer in my strange
new body curving
to breast and hip, I laughed
at tourists who remembered
the headlines, expected
to find whale bone
and ash, those strangers
who didn't know
the ocean had washed
the beach flat and clean again.

whale beaching 1979
written 1992

Words and Breath

I: Suzanne: 1976

That summer
you came to visit
from Arkansas,
long–time friend
of my parents:

You stayed a week, swam
the river, clambered up
Battle Rock with me.
You and your woman lover.

That summer they say
the county sheriff beat
a hitchhiker almost to death, a thin
white man with long hair
and a guitar, then laughed
faggot all over town.

I showed you
muskrat, deer, the best
blackberry bramble, asked you
to come live with me
in my river valley.
Parents grew silent:
the word *lesbian*
hovered and fell.

You must have waited
until our house slept,
milky way splayed
across the sky,
to hold hands, let
fingers trail belly and hip.

II: Main Street: 1982

I left that valley, found
women in the city, words
and breath, touch and taste,
walked the streets as if
they were logging roads.

> Still, the women at the bank
> know me by name, their husbands
> pull crab, fill their boats
> with snapper and cod
> when the chinook aren't running.

> Main Street from the pizza parlor
> to Pitch's Tavern, past
> the Kar Kare Klinic, I watch
> for small ineffable signs: hair
> trimmed short, single
> silver stud, left hand,
> no rings. Watch and wait.

> An hour north, Sunday
> is gay night at Lucky's,
> only the fishermen
> want a fight.
> No one dances close.

III: River Rock: 1987

I study
a map, follow
the rumors,
rain, streambed
curving north,
drive beyond
the familiar
clearcuts.

Trees gray green,
winter light:

I used to say
I found dykes
with faces clear,
hair spiked, old smell
of cedar and garlic.

But that
was always
too simple.

I stay
long enough
to hike
the logging roads,
split firewood,
sleep alone.

Over dinner
we lean
into each other.

I've forgotten the stories
but not how they knocked
one against another,
river rock underfoot.

coming out as a dyke 1976–1987
written 1991, 2007

In the City

I walk the streets as if they were logging roads. Lose myself in the maze of stoplights, one-way streets, skyscrapers. *In the backwoods I shot seagulls at the county dump. Cut bear claws apart, traced tendon and ligament.* And here I gawk. Homeless people, their shopping carts and bedrolls. Black people. Chinese people. Chicanos. Drag queens and punks. Vets down on Burnside Avenue. Gawk at them all. *We used to drown stray cats, gunny sacks tied tight, weighted with rock. The ones we didn't drown we skinned naked to look like infants hung from their heels.* The white men in their wool suits, limos shined to sparkle. I gawk. Take alleyways past garbage cans rolling loose, dumpsters overflowing, smell of rain and piss on concrete. Suck in the thick weave of Spanish, Cantonese, street talk, English. Screech, wail, pierce of ambulance, fire truck, squad car. *We played chicken, 60 miles an hour on the backroads, our first funerals.* I learn to count blocks, memorize parallel and perpendicular, remember not to nod and smile at every passerby crossing Broadway. I don't want to believe all the rules have changed.

living in Portland 1982
written 1994

East Oakland

Old photographs: your hair
straight, parted, curled
at the ends. Mouth tight,
eyes refuse the camera.
I wouldn't have
recognized you then

and now you lean against
the door frame laughing, short
short afro, broad smile.

East Oakland, 1965:
your brothers in and out
of jail, gun fights down
the street, and every morning
your mama straightened your hair,
burning the back of your neck.

You tip your chair back,
hands crossed behind head,
watch your reflection
in the night–black window.
You say *my daddy
always sits like this.*

I want to twirl you
across the room,
my hand light
on the small
of your back, want
our bodies to catch
the rhythm, words
never ceasing.

You write:
At first
we held hands
like children
who bravely choose partners.

Then tell me: *my second year*
of college I took a field trip, busload
of white kids and me. We drove down
96th Avenue, right past the house
I grew up in, its square yard. Home
called ghetto for the first time.

And me, that white town
I call home, the rumors persist:
north of Bald Mountain, a lynching
tree, just follow the logging roads.

My tremors travel
through the arc of our walk,
hands swing into rhythm,
your palm cool and dry,
subway to 54th Street,
words never ceasing.

They taunted me *weirdo, retard,*
monkey, hey lezzie. Taunted you—
you don't say the words. I spread
my body against yours, try
to imagine East Oakland, 1965.

Later I walk you to your car,
steady my hand in yours,
count the tremors.

relationship 1985
written 1992

Tremors

Hands burled and knobby, I tuck them
against my body, let tremors run
from shoulder blade to fingertip. Tension
burns the same track of muscles, pencil slows
across blue-lined paper, words scratch
like sandpiper tracks at low tide.
Kids call cripple. Bank tellers stare silent.
Doctors predict arthritis. Joints crack
in the vise grip: my hands want
to learn to swear.
                    Late at night
as I trace the long curve of your body,
tremors touch skin, reach inside,
and I expect to be taunted, only to have you
rise beneath my hands, ask for more.

everyday encounters
written 1992

Interlude II: Updraft

Tell it as a memory, a dream, a story: once I stood in front of my sister and asked, "Do I look like a boy or a girl?" I couldn't see myself in the mirror.

And how will you tell it? Maybe you played hop-scotch and jump rope with the girls, while the boys taunted, words falling like fists and rocks. Maybe you fell asleep hoping beyond hope that you'd wake up a girl, a boy, something right. Maybe the boys let you play flag football and secret forts until your breasts appeared. Whatever the stories, haul them up by the handful, but don't tell them as if they were simple. Where do the breaks, ruptures, contradictions, repetitions live? The marrow twists and turns, tangling toward the sun, never symmetrical, a shadblow tree.

I flew my kite for hours on end, spinning line out, red tail hawks keening on the updrafts, sun and wind reaching through me.

written 2005–2007

Last Refrain

Two–years–old, arms
reach up a circle,
red hair spread
against white sheet,
eyelashes curl: I sleep
easy girl–child sleep—

this last refrain
before he pushes
his way into me,
hands wrapped tight,

before I learn
sleep like a fist,
a drug, a stone,

sleep so hard I'll tell
the women who share
my bed to wake me
if ever the house burns

otherwise I will
burn with it.

Subway stops
they'll call
hey red, hey red,

and body will know:
watch knees,
throat, eyes,
not groin.

For years we'll live,
my father and I,
python and prey.

Leap, spin, twirl,
thin night air:

the 1 a.m. train arrives.
To home and sleep.

childhood 1965, adulthood 1984
written 1992, 2007

Bruises

My brother built pipe bombs,
collected racing bikes, and sailed

the north wind, school to home
every day, seven miles in 15 minutes.

He and I could have fed each other
salmonberries, huckleberries, clover–sweet

milk. My sister, her feet creased
with dirt and tough—gravel, thistle, briar—

inhabited a make–believe world.
We could have tended the bruises,

warmed each other in tall
spiky grass. And I.

I wanted to be a hermit like some girls
want to be cowboys. Bodies festooned.

Brother's laugh, sister's grace.
We could have but didn't.

childhood 1974–1980
written 1996

No Longer Small and Lonely

Who if not the girl? The butch who changes her name, shaves her head, binds her breasts, who wants to live without a pronoun, called sir, son, young man, dressed in suits sharply pressed. The queer one who grew up not girl, not boy, riding the wind bareback. The guy who shapes his body, chest flat, beard finally growing, who stands in the mirror ready. The boy who flew his kite in the hayfields, never wanting to go home. My arms yearned to be that tug on the other end of the kite string.

The boy who dreamed: last night I lay down at the dense dark edge of joy. We talked for hours, tracking the moon. I swallowed its smell, licked the length of its body, rolled my muscled skin into its shaggy coat, and woke not remembering. I slept a small, lonely child inside thick dreamless sleep.

Take your pillow and favorite quilt, walk down into the fields freshly mown. Who if not girl, boy, child?

I dreamed of walking—feet to earth, skin to granite. A gentle rhythm of left, right, left again, arms swinging loose. A fierce pull up the north face, switchback to ridgeline. A long stride from home to work every morning. A slow meander through the woods. I learned to walk on shaky feet, a gimp whose heels refused to reach the ground. I wore big blocky shoes and practiced my balance, as focused as a dancer learning to spot.

Dreamed of walking across the country. During lunch recess, Mary and I conjured how we'd start in Bangor, Maine, end in Newport, Oregon, follow the back roads, pitch our tent in cow pastures and backyards, 3,000 miles from sea to shining sea. We walked endless laps around the ball field repeating this plan, detail upon detail, until a decade later I had graduated from college, and she had dropped out to work at Hardees, and between us we had a thousand dollars and a road map. I left my first girlfriend; she left her best drinking buddies; we caught a midnight Greyhound to Bangor. It didn't last. Thirty-five soggy miles of walking, we stopped at a roadside diner, ate cheeseburgers, fries, and apple pie à la mode. As Mary paid our bill, the waitress asked, cocking her head toward me, "Is he your husband?" We stood in the gravel parking lot, our gear wet, feet blistered, and she gave up. I was the rain that fell between us.

> Lay your bed clothes down, curl under them, and watch stars spread white across the valley, your eyes growing wide and wider, night no longer a simple black but full of its own color, until you swallow the Milky Way into your sleep. Who if not girl, boy, child, gimp, rain?

Not long after, I joined a peace march and walked 3,700 miles from L.A. to D.C. Once every three weeks a bomb exploded deep in the desert; they called it nuclear testing. The U.S. spent billions of dollars designing a leaky umbrella; they called it the space defense initiative. The military stockpiled weapons; they called them peacemaker, patriot, cruise. Missile silos dotted the prairie. We flooded the country, a river in protest.

While I dreamed of walking, my father dreamed of sailing around the world. My father—rapist, sadist, crazy man. He used all the weapons he owned, except his shotgun. Cracked my body wide open. Stole my heart. Shut the door. Locked it tight. I swam, a chinook upstream.

> *Wake up in the dew–drenched dark to coyotes howling, dogs wailing the harmony, sky even denser with stars, body nestled into ten thousand dreams. Who if not girl, boy, child, gimp, rain, river, chinook?*

He talked about building a boat, sanding and varnishing the hull, rigging its sail, and heading west. He drew the plans, spent long hours in his woodshop, built chairs, tables, bookshelves, cabinets, even a house. His hands were ridged with veins, small blue tributaries branching up his arms. He sanded walnut, cherry, maple until it gleamed, soaking the grain with linseed oil, wood turning the color of honey, chocolate, fresh baked bread, texture of silk. But he never started his boat, never cut the plywood, steamed the ribs, checked the mast for true. Instead he drank cheap white wine and read endlessly about Marco Polo, Christopher Columbus, Ferdinand Magellan, Sir Francis Drake, those men who sailed the world so long ago. Drunk, my father became an almost harmless man, a white man who only occasionally grabbed at my body. I rose transparent as heat off a hot, hot bath.

My rapist the dreamer, I learned thick dreamless sleep from him. He took my sleeping, twisted it like an arm until it broke. Middle of the night, whatever inexplicable misery he had planned for me, I came a small, lonely child, roused from sleep, body warm and pliable. And later blood wiped off lips, semen mopped from thighs, wrists and ankles untied, pajamas slipped back on, I returned to sleep, the night's terror becoming my dream, my dreams slipping over the edge. Mornings after, I woke, self returning to self, ate my oatmeal, went to school, played tetherball and four square at recess, as if nothing had happened. I grew, a berry bramble untouchable. I didn't dream for 30 years.

> And when you wake next, wind and sun pushing at your skin, you won't remember any of the details, not the coyotes, not the stars, not the wild dream sex, only that your body is fuller than it's ever been. Who if not girl, boy, child, gimp, rain, river, chinook, heat, bramble?

The man I used to call father, let him tumble forever. I have stormed his bunker, picked the lock, found my heart amidst the rubble, laughed him off the edge of the world.

No longer small and lonely, I live among the furious and joyful. We dance, sing, drum, limp, roll, walk, swish, howl our way though the world. The next 10,000 miles await, wild open of sky. I'll no longer pretend, no longer be afraid: neither girl nor boy, I am a boulder that splits the current and dreams.

coming out as genderqueer 1993–1997, peace walk 1986 written 1998

Sleep

tonight she goes
to the belly   wraps herself
in morning sugar pine
light   swallow swoop
dusk light   river narrows
to current   call and response
high summer hay
season   air drifts
sweet chafe   vultures
circle updraft down
gorge on mice   rabbits
voles caught in mowing
machines   bones coming
clean   lichen   moss   soft
sponge of rotten log
fawn–spotted   dapple
before reaching
dark bottom

beginning to dream 1994
written 1996

Arriving

Late November, the woodpile a chaos, I remove my
hat, roll up my sleeves and stack—round by round,
three rows deep, shoulder high—birch, maple, oak.
Back arches, stretches, and hours later I turn, lake
half frozen. Find the line between ice and water,
water and far shore, hill and sky.

\ \ \ \ \

No longer nightmare, daytime
terror: this dream arrives,
clap of thunder,
herd of horses,
tumble of agates.

    They appear, three old women sitting in a
    stone house. My grandmothers.

This dream arrives, a cacophony
of color leaping from ankle
to knee. Let this too
be a mark, a sign, an omen.

    They know me as Eli River.

No longer vigil or rage:
this dream sings an old name,
new name, child
who splits the current.

They send me beyond the trees, grasses, abandoned orchard.

This dream swims a sun–dappled
bottom, lithe and fast—
prayers, vows, promises
breathe underwater.

\ \ \ \ \

Long ago I left the ocean, river, berry bramble, fox-
glove, wild rhododendron, left for good. I lost not
only the stories in my pockets, warmed to my body
heat, but also the pockets themselves.

\ \ \ \ \

This dream arrives,
frog nestled
on ankle, black spots,
orange skin, and poison—

strong enough
to numb hands,
slow hearts.

They direct me to a tattoo parlor.

No longer hallucination
or memory: pigment enters
skin. Imagine
a long–bodied leap.

Insist I'll never belong to any one place.

This dream arrives
twined in silver
and rock, sweet smell
of another human body.

Not one place but many—tree, water, land. You'll
belong to the world.

Comes angled
across the current, crouched
in the eddies—frog, heron, crane.
Listen for the downbeat.

\\\\\

And as I turn toward the lake, woodpile much small-
er, chips hanging on my shirt, for a moment I belong
to this waning day, belong to an old name, new
name, to many places all at once.

naming myself 1997
written 1997–2007

Clothes

From my closet, I pull black twill trousers and a white dress shirt, narrow black belt and burgundy tie. I start with a clean undershirt, wrap my breasts tight against chest.

I'm in the middle of a love affair with ties. I find myself at the mall, ostensibly shopping for sheets or towels, but really I'm there just to check out the ties, touch the trail of silk patterns displayed at Hudson's, Sears, the Men's Wearehouse. Find myself in the jumble of
secondhand stores, searching for the narrowest of black ties, textured with thin diagonal lines. A serious love affair.

I finish buttoning my shirt. Slip tie under collar, cross the two ends, pulling the wide one up and over, through the second loop. Draw the knot close to my neck, leave a dimple exactly right. I adore how I look after I've shrugged into my blazer, put on dress shoes, tie flat and smooth against shirt, curve of breast and hip vanishing under clothes.

Dream: Greyhound bus station, women's washroom. I look at myself in the mirror, notice that I'm growing a beard, golden hair curling against skin. Pull my hands through the sunlight, happy but puzzled, because I know I have not yet started taking testosterone.

For most of my life I have hated clothes and hated shopping for them even more. I remember the trips.

My mother and I drive our beat–up VW van 65 miles to the nearest shopping center. She sets the agenda. First, we go to the fabric store where she leafs through pattern books, pointing at line drawings, asking, "Do you like this? What about that?" asking as if I care. How am I to choose between one ugly dress and another? I simply try to avoid lace and ruffles. Then we look for cloth, my mother sorting through the bolts to find just the right fabric at just the right price. She has no love affair with—or talent for—sewing. Rather, this is a strategy to save money, to clothe me and my siblings on a budget already stretched thin. After the fabric store, we walk to Penny's to buy socks and underwear. I always make a beeline to the boys' department to look at flannel shirts, finger stiff denim jeans, my mother tracking me down, leading me back to the girls' racks.

Later with money of my own, I bought jeans and t–shirts, which I wore to rags, baggier the better. Clothes were to hide in, to tent over my body. I didn't want anyone calling me pretty.

But now as I begin to pull into my body, inhabit this house of bone and muscle, I have also started to lust after tuxedo jackets and black, rayon–backed vests, crisp oxford shirts and silver tie tacks. Started to pay attention to how I like my jeans baggy off the hip, my flannel shirts buttery soft. I find myself tucking my shirt in, wearing a wide leather belt, polishing my boots. I want girls to notice, boys to flirt.

returning to my body 1996–2000
written 1998–2007

Interlude III: Reverberate

Spinning line out, five hundred feet, a thousand, I wanted a name for every rock, tree, grass, fish.

\\\\\

But now, kite flyer turned poet, tell me: whose stories, what communities, which histories do you choose, and how is your choosing shaped? Tell me: the food that fills your belly; the roof that shelters your sleep; the white skin that protects your body; the secure job that pays your bills, buys your books, music, vacations. This too is a map: a telling where bombs don't fall nor roads explode, where soldiers don't come pounding door–to–door; a specific time and place whether spoken or not. Tell me: a willful unknowing or a reckoning of privilege. Tell me.

\\\\\

Spinning line out, I listened to the hills echo, keen, reverberate, cradling the red tail's lonely call.

written 2005–2007

Blackberries

Tongues and hands stained,
seeds caught like sweet
sand between our teeth,
                my brother
and I used to have berry
fights. Purple black
explosions covered
our bodies,
           not bruises, not
this time. Brambles drooped jeweled,
sun–soaked berries nearly
bursting even before
we picked them.
              And now years
later in the desert, watching
bombers fly practice runs,
I imagine grenades exploding
like blackberries.

childhood 1977
written 1992

The Stories Mama Tells

I.

Elizabeth, my preemie baby,
you rode 36 hours
of labor, quickly learned
to scream.

The same stories
over and over: glass box
called incubator, called
home, I know
where Mama will pause—

They didn't let me
touch you for a month.

Where she will smile—*Sarah,*
you were born into a January storm,
snow gripping your father's beard,
beginning to cover the car—

I can picture it:
cave of steel
lit by the only
street lamp in town—
He handed you
to me, umbilical cord
still connected.
Gesture big
with her hands—

Nick, you arrived,
birth sac still
unbroken—

a landscape submerged
in fog. I imagine
the doctor breaking that gray
amorphous film, unveiling
my brother to morning light.

From her I learned the words
  birth accident ovarian cyst
  surgery oxygen
  deprivation induced labor
  premature
  birth   birth accident.

II.

I have one story I never
meant to tell, a patchwork
of medical records:

I was 24 and poor
when the doctor found the cyst, tiny
tiny balanced against my ovary, he said
nothing. Three years later,
four weeks pregnant, seed
of a child hanging there too,
he told me to drink milk.

I never saw him again:
simple—no milk money,
no doctor money, no insurance.
Followed my new husband
to his new job halfway
across the country, never guessed
I was growing twins.
Took up housekeeping
in the backwoods, tried
to forget Detroit. Six months pregnant
I went to another doctor.
He felt the twins: one
with a heart, its steady thump,
and the other, a swelling bag.
He too said nothing except
"I'll see you in three weeks."

The twins gripped each other,
wrestled in the dark cave
of my insides. The doctor said, "Jane,
I have bad news." Cut me open,
plucked death away bloomed big
as a melon, threw it
in the dumpster. You were
the other twin born
a week later,
not much bigger.

III.

Elizabeth,
those words: disabled
handicapped
crippled   deformed
I hated them all.

Tried to pretend
you didn't have
cerebral palsy, prayed
for a miracle cure, refused
to teach you the woodlore
of bitterness.

IV.

Over coffee, beer,
bread and lentil soup,
stories get told.
Listen, Mama:

> *I signed a release*
> *as I went under,*
> *woke up not knowing*
> *they had tied my tubes.*

Nick and I spent a childhood
catching frogs, climbing
trees, but now
we're enclosed again
in glass and fog.

> *That last course*
> *of electric shock, whole decades*
> *just disappeared, there's no more*
> *remembering.*

Round–bellied little girl, Sarah would dance
in the kitchen all afternoon to *Swan Lake.*

The doctor put me on
three years of diets, and still
the tumor weighed
47 pounds
when he finally
removed it.

She used to place her body
between me and the kids
throwing rocks.

They keep adding
a "Do Not Resuscitate" order
to my chart, even though
I've been clear, "If ever I stop breathing,
use all your technology."

V.

You were never
the only one.

But still I wonder:
if the doctors
had been honest,
if my hands
didn't shake, if I hadn't
grown up
to the word *cripple*.

birth 1963
written 1992

Psych Ward in Three Voices

when i wake
flailing out
of nightmare
please feed me
applesauce

the voices

Never high sweet notes of joy,
shrinks call them auditory hallucinations.

feed me applesauce
covered with cream
thick cinnamon brown
chunks of gravenstein apple

I watch them fill your head,
cajole, convince, command.

the voices rumble

let me remember
mama's kitchen
that cinnamon mud
simmering as she
cored and cut apples

the voices roar it's time

I tuck oven–warmed towels
around your feet.

mama sang to herself
as she ladled the sauce
into clear ball jars

    I sit with you
    as the iv drips.

        hurricane in my head

in the winter
she filled my bowl
with warm applesauce

        the voices rage it's time—time to go

    Tie one history to the next,
    dream to torture.

        rumble roar ravish

still humming
she would cover
the sauce with
cold jersey cream

        glimpse gravity gone

    Memory to starvation,
    I grasp the knots.

hospitalization 1992
written 1992, 2007

Bedrock

Night after night I finger
each thin cable of story,

first–born preemie
you lived too long
in a glass box
that october of '63

twine them together, the details to which
no one will dance: a hundred sleeping pills

blue as eggshell, fifth of whiskey.
I let the bottles float away, lay down to wait.

Words fold one on top
of another, page after page.

November 15, 1986, Lincoln Memorial. Tonight we
have finished 3,700 miles. I can already feel the reality
of walking L.A. to Vegas, Denver to Omaha, Chicago to
Cleveland, Harrisburg to Harlem, Philly to D.C., begin
to slip. Our last rally, we circle the reflecting pool. In
the dark our bodies become simple outlines, each a
candle. The small flames waver on the black surface. I
don't want to stop.

I sleep with you under my pillow,
walk with you under my tongue.

You have broken my teeth, bruised
my gums. My small gray stone.

\\\\\

For years I've struggled to find words, lines, stanzas
to tell you about torture. A language you might
believe—metaphor wrapping around terror, elision
breaking the already broken, meter catching the pure
dizzy whirl. A language I might be able to utter. Today
Adrianne said, "Don't write it pretty."

\\\\\

River knee hip shoulder deep.
I fell away, a sack of stones.

April 11, 1986, Nevada Test Site. News of a test just
detonated came over the shortwave an hour ago. I've
been sitting at the barbed wire fence ever since,
watching the desert, Tonapah Mountains to my back,
creosote in full bloom. I keep expecting to feel shock
waves. Tom sits upwind of me, smoking his pipe. I
can't stop crying. All of a sudden he's gone, rolled
under the fence to walk a few illegal steps. I almost
join him.

you would scoot yourself
into a corner   jam your head
against the glass   and scream.
I woke up, not dead, still waiting,
walked home so drunk

I'll never remember. Late afternoon, water striders
rest in the shadows, legs dimpling the surface.

April 17, 1986, 15 miles east of Vegas. I dream of a
woman who shaves her head bald, carves ghost–like
petroglyphs into her skull. She and I are lovers. We
walk to ground zero. Wait for the bombs to be tested
under our feet. Camp in their craters. I wake to
desert sun filling my tent.

one day as i stood at the door
watching you   the ward nurse
came by   said i always know
which ones will live

Tension and grip, the living balanced
against the dead—boulder hopping

in the North Cascades: back leg
reaches, front leg bends, body weight

follows—balance lives in the space
between muscle and earth.

I know you read the stories, recognize the names—
Pinochet, P.W. Botha, Samoza—and the places—
Guantanamo Bay, Abu Ghraib. But the list doesn't
stop there; you need to add my grandfather the
gravedigger. He knew how to use electrodes, taped
them to the soles of my feet, palms of my hands,
small of my back. My grandmother led me to and
from that basement room. My father learned from
them, measured the blood, held me down. In an ear-
lier draft, I cut the lines about torture, couldn't find
the right mix of hallucination and horror.

\\\\\

Body comes unmoored, floating
free, they wrapped me in warm towels,

poured charcoal down my stomach,
asked questions too many to count.

i couldn't take my eyes
off you   head covered
with peach fuzz   the ward nurse
said   your baby she'll live   she's a fighter

July 6, 1986, Strategic Air Command, Nebraska. I
watch counter–demonstrators burn a Soviet flag.
Flames gnaw through the red background, up and
over the yellow sickle. They call us commie dykes. We
laugh and shrug.

I live on a road, cobbled and gray,
never know which way it will lead:
graveyard of memory or river
at dusk Not balance but war.

\\\\\

Electrodes taped in place and then? Which verbs
might suffice: *surge, radiate, scream, pulse, jolt?* As if
the eternity that coursed down my spine were water,
light, sound, heartbeat, earthquake. Riverbed of pain.
Tell me: is this too pretty?

\\\\\

First day on the psych ward, I washed
my hair, tugging at the knots,

vomit flecked eggshell blue.
I am the child.

a week later   the doctor pulled
the tubes from your nose
unplugged the iv   let me hold you

October 17, 1986, Allentown, Pennsylvania. I walk the
last three miles into camp with a man just off work,
suit jacket flung over one shoulder, black leather
shoes clicking the pavement. He asks the usual questions about the Walk, then we talk disarmament, the
Reagan–Gorbachev summit, the Soviet moratorium
on nuclear testing, the budget for SDI. We disagree,
choose not to argue, don't talk about Hiroshima,
Chernobyl, the Bikini atolls, the Downwinders.

The child they turned to glass and stone.
The shrinks feed me anti–psychotics.

Will you call me crazy? Turn away? Talk about false
memory syndrome? Act surprised when it's not only
dictators, military *juntas*, and Pentagon goons who
have learned routines of torture, but also priests,
Klansmen, neo–Nazis, and guys down the street?
Listen: too many of us have waited, hands and feet
bound, fed the fire, listened to the screams, huddled
against the bars. You can choose to ignore and deny
it. I envy that choice. Or you can come walk the distance.

\\\\\\

Each thin cable and soon I will have
a rope, strong and thick, to anchor here

in the bedrock, stretch high across
the river, beginnings of a bridge.

dealing with ritual abuse 1992–2002
written 1996, 2007

Camped at 12 Mile Beach, Lake Superior

Nick, each morning I wake,
expecting to smell
salt, seaweed, our cold
cold ocean.

Brother of blackberry
bramble and skipping stones,
I wait for the roar
of surf, seals glinting black.

You would understand:
this lake is not
familiar enough
even as the water
numbs my feet.

> *when the watermelon come ripe*
> *and cicadas drum the fields*

Brother of my homesickness,
early half-ripe apples and late
afternoon swims: you were
11 when I left,
a boy grown tall.
You lived with our father,
river and rock, learned
not to speak.

when cicadas drum the fields
and we break the rind

This fall with Iraq
in the headlines, do you
talk military strategy,
joke about Arab terrorists,
hang a flag from your front porch?

Or do you join the protests,
sign the petitions, ready to flee
if ever the draft comes round again,
no longer Canada, but south?

when we break the rind
and eat the fruit in chunks

Down my block, the neighbors grow
organic vegetables, refuse
their taxes, and I
haunt the streets. Brother
of my homesickness,

when we eat the fruit in chunks
and juice streaks our shirts

will you be called in,
sent to the naval base in San Diego
where the ocean is warm,
then Saudi Arabia?
I wait, haven't read
the news in a week,
bluff caves to beach:
ocean is never
this quiet.

when juice streaks our shirts
do we leave having tasted hope

first gulf war 1991
written 1992, 2007

Interlude IV: Reach

With whom do we break the bone open? And once broken, what does the telling take; how do we shift those stories across language, culture, community? And once translated, who listens and how?

\\\\\

Years ago I studied the work of Russian poet Anna Akhmatova. She wrote political poems through Stalin's long reign and lived for several decades under house arrest. I don't know a single word of Russian, and so reading her in translation was a gift, a door unlocked.

One day in the library, I went looking for as many different versions of her poem "Requiem" as I could find. I pulled them off the shelves, sat down at a big wooden table, and laid them out side–by–side. I studied late, examining line breaks, slant rhyme, meter; searching for the one exact translation to offer me the original, unmediated poem. I didn't succeed. How could any single translation catch all the layers: depth of word, reach of metaphor, rocking of sound and rhythm? Without knowing Russian, all I had were four or five overlapping poems, each anchored in some way to the original, each bridging a distance, each a door unlocked but not held wide.

\\\\\

Our telling reaches across chasms of power and privilege. Struggles with willful unknowing. Stands on *fault lines between people most similar. Insists upon wholeness. This is the work of translation.*

All too often, it's exhausting, as we repeat our most familiar stories, only to have them heard as freakish, exotic, inspirational. Or it's simply frustrating and slow, however necessary. But sometimes, it's revelatory, the tug of a kite, sun and wind reaching through.

written 2005–2007

Scars

I pour a bath, dissolve a handful of mineral salts, catching each crystal in the stream of hot water, crack a window, try to light the candles. They float in a bowl of water, and as I touch match to wick, my hand jumps, tremor climbing the ladder of my arm. I swamp one candle, then the other, give up. Strip my clothes—t–shirt, high tops, jeans, boxers. Pull off my binder, breasts coming free. I think about the not–so–long–ago laws against cross–dressing, about old–time butches and the price they paid. Their stories of bar raids, strip searches, jail cells scare me.

Heat stings. Right arm loosens, body buoyant. Tremors rock water, no longer locked in shoulder and back. I finger the appendectomy scar stretched from navel to pubic hair, a thick, ropy trail cut down my center. Cup the knobby glob of tissue on my right knee, remnants of one fall among thousands. Trace the ridged line across my left palm, mark of a chisel slipping from wood to flesh.

Except for that thick ropy braid, my scars don't come from a surgeon's scalpel, an unusual circumstance for anyone physically disabled since birth. My quad muscles were never cut, sewn back together. Achilles tendons, never severed. Pins, never inserted into hips and knees. The bodies of disabled people so often end up criss–crossed with scars, childhoods punctuated by surgery. But not mine: my skin didn't become a map. For that, I need to go subterranean. Muscles knotted, tendons inflamed, vertebrae too sore to touch.

As I soak, wind picks up outside, tosses cedars and firs into a whispery dance. I submerge myself, tremor dissolved into hot water. Look down at my breasts. One day I may have scars to trace here: not the matted tissue of a radical mastectomy, hoping against hope cancer won't return; but rather the feathery lines of a chest reconstructed to follow the ridge of pectoral muscle, surgery gladly chosen. Sometimes this is what I want, curve of breast irrevocably gone. But will I let the doctors, scalpels in hand, touch my skin? Will I have enough desire, enough courage, enough money?

> *Dream: I lie on top of him, my left leg pressed between his, can feel his cock bulging there against my thigh. We have taken off only our shoes. Kissing slow, talking slow, I want to slide my hands up under his shirt, up to rest along his shoulder blades. Turn him over, his body arching into my weight, cup his balls in one hand, and take him gently. I want to but don't. Instead we're kissing with all our clothes between us. I tell him, "If you want to be lovers with me, you need to know: on the streets we will be faggots, and in bed we will not forget."*

Underwater I touch the tub, white porcelain. Touch my skin, tropical tree frogs tattooed up my leg—orange, green, red, yellow. When people ask, I say, "I dreamed them in vivid, living color, and the dream wouldn't leave me alone." Touch myself, soft and warm. None of my scars come from a cop's billy club.

returning to my body 1996–2007
written 1998, 2007

To the Curious People Who Ask, "What Do Your Tremors Feel Like?"

Tell me: have you ever watched
hands play a piano? Fingers
on the keys, ivory to skin, dance
white to black and back again, run
wild and loose, thump and caress
the universe cradled inside
a baby grand, those hands
I lost at birth. Breath squeezed
to empty gasps, I fell into the world,
brain of my fingers half dead.
Explain to me your hands resting
still as water before they dance.
That I cannot imagine.

after being asked yet again about my tremors 1990
written 1992

Retard, Cripple, Defect

If only we had taken
the boys on, those
who knew the litany best—
rocks and erasers,
bruising words. Instead
the taunted turned:
her paper-thin voice reached
across the school yard, my shaky
fists answered back.
Lonely bodies, we were
the only two.

grade school 1975
written 1994

Gawking, Gaping, Staring

Gawking, gaping, staring: I can't say when it first happened. When first a pair of eyes caught me, held me in their vice grip, tore skin from muscle, muscle from bone. Those eyes always shouted, "Freak, retard, cripple," demanded an answer for tremoring hands, a tomboy's bold and unsteady gait I never grew out of. It started young, anywhere I encountered strangers. Gawking, gaping, staring seeped into my bones, became the marrow. I spent 30 years shutting it out, slamming the door.

> *The gawkers never get it right, but what I want to know is this: will you? When my smile finds you across the room, will you notice the odd angle of my wrists cocked and decide I am a pane of glass to look right through? Or will you smile back?*

I come from people who have long histories of being on stage—freaks and drag queens, court jesters and scientific experiments. Sometimes we've been proud, other times just desperate. We've posed for anthropologists and cringed in front of doctors, performed the greatest spectacles and thumbed our noses at the shadow called *normal*. The gawkers used to pay good money; now they get in for free.

\\\\\

Being on stage is dangerous. Just ask Khoi woman Saartje Baartman, exhibited as the Hottentot Venus. She paced a cage on demand and posed for French naturalists. After she died, her genitals became a museum display for over a century. I listen to the histories and everywhere hear the words *freak, savage.*

$$\setminus\setminus\setminus\setminus$$

The gawkers think I'm deaf or "mentally retarded." They think I'm a 20–year–old guy or a middle–aged butch. They can't make up their minds, start with sir, end with ma'am, waver in the middle. They think I'm that pane of glass.

I spent so many years shutting the staring out. Friends would ask, "Did you see that person gaping at you?" and I'd answer, "What person?" It's a great survival strategy but not very selective. In truth the door slammed hard, and I lost it all, all the appreciation, flirtation, solidarity, that can be wrapped into a gaze.

I couldn't imagine anyone, much less a lover, reaching beneath my clothing, beneath all the ugly words, beneath my shame and armor, eyes and hands returning me to grace, beauty, passion.

Never imagined this: *He cradles my right hand against his body and says, "Your tremors feel so good." And says, "I can't get enough of your shaky touch." And says, "I love your cerebral palsy."* Shame and disbelief flood my body, drowning his words. How do I begin to learn his lustful gaze?

$$\setminus\setminus\setminus\setminus$$

Being on stage is an act of faith. Just ask William Johnson. African–American and cognitively disabled, he stepped up to the freak stage; donned an ape costume and shaved his head, save for a tuft of hair at the very top; became the monkey man, the missing link, the "What–Is–It." He died a rich man, affectionately known by his co–workers as the "dean of freaks." But he could have just as easily been a lonely, frightened man, coerced, bullied, trapped by freak show owners and managers. I listen to the histories and everywhere hear the words *savage, defect.*

\\\\\

These days I practice gawking at the gawkers; it's an act of resistance. If I had a time machine, I'd travel back to the freak show. Sneak in after hours, after all the folks who worked long days selling themselves as armless wonders and wild savages had stepped off their platforms, out of their geek pits, from behind their curtains. I'd walk among them—the fat women, the short–statured men, the folks without legs, the supposed half–men/half women, the conjoined twins, the bearded women, the snake charmers and sword swallowers—as they took off their costumes, washed their faces, sat down to dinner. I'd gather their words, their laughter, their scorn at the rubes who bought their trinkets and believed half their lies. I'd breathe their fierceness into me.

The gawkers have turned away from me, laughed, thrown rocks, pointed their fingers, quoted bible verses, called me immoral and depraved, tried to heal me, swamped me in pity. Their hatred snarls into me.

They never get it right, but what I want to know is this: will you? If I touch you with tremoring hands, will you wince away, thinking cripple, thinking ugly? Or will you unfold to my body, let my trembling shimmer beneath your skin?

I practice overt resistance and unabashed pride, flirting as hard as I know how. On the Castro, I check out the bears, big burly men with full beards and open shirts. One of them catches my eyes. I hold his gaze for a single moment too long, watch as it slips down my body. He asks, "Are you a boy or a girl?" not taunting but curious. I don't answer, walk away smiling, skin warm.

In another world at another time, I would have grown up neither boy nor girl, but something entirely different. In English there are no good words, no easy words. All I have is the shadowland of neither man nor woman, a suspension bridge tethered between negatives. One day we may have a language to take us to a place that is neither masculine nor feminine, day nor night, mortise nor tenon. But for now, what could I possibly say to the bears cruising me at 3 p.m. as sunlight streams over concrete?

\\\\\

Being on stage is risky. Just ask Billy Tipton. He worked the jazz stage with his piano, saxophone, and comedy routines; lived for 50 years as a female–bodied man; married five times; and had three sons. The gawking started after his death as the headlines roared, "Jazz Musician Spent Life Concealing Fantastic Secret." I listen to the histories and everywhere hear the words defect, queer.

\\\\\

It usually only takes one long glance at the gawkers—kids on their way home from school, old women with their grocery bags, young professionals dressed for work—one unflinching glance in return. But before they turn away, I want someone to tell me just once what they're staring at. My tremoring hands? My red hair? My broad, off–center stance, shoulders well–muscled and lopsided? My slurred speech? Just once. But typically one steely glance, and they're gone.

There is a freak show photo: Hiram and Barney Davis off stage—small, wiry men, white, cognitively disabled, raised in Ohio. They wear goatees, hair falling past their shoulders; look mildly and directly into the camera. On–stage, they played "Waino and Plutano, the wild men from Borneo," snapped, snarled, growled, shook their chains at the audience. Rubes paid good money to come watch. I hope that sometimes they stopped mid–performance, up there on the sideshow platform, and stared back, turning their mild and direct gaze to the rubes, gawking at the gawkers.

They never get it right, but what I want to know is this: will you? When I walk through the world, will you simply scramble for the correct pronoun? Or will you imagine a river at dusk, its skin smooth and unbroken, sun no longer braided into sparkles?

Cliff divers hurl their bodies from fifty feet, neither flying nor earth–bound, three somersaults and a half turn, entering the water free–fall without a ripple. Will you get it right?

I'm taking Hiram and Barney as my teachers and looking for the places where staring finally turns to something else, something true to the bone. Where strength is softened and tempered, love honed and stretched. Where gender is more than a simple binary. Where we encourage each other to swish and swagger, limp and roll, and learn the language of pride. Places where our bodies become home. Gawking, gaping, staring: I can't say when it first happened.

freak show 1800s, everyday encounters
written 2002–2007

Interlude V: Demand

Certainly it's necessary to tell it: I used to fly my kite for hours on end. And still today I can feel its tug, beckon of sky and wind. But by itself, story isn't enough.

We need to tell, talk, translate the marrow. Tell it as trouble—all the years of whispers, snickers, earnest questions, "Do you know this is the women's restroom?" Tell it as joy—the first time your body felt alive and supple. Talk it as postmodern theory, teasing those ideas out of the bramble, or as a training for health–care providers. Translate it as history, policy, fierceness, rebellion, civil rights, a poem sung in the streets.

Let story be that kite, wild blue of sky, tug and beckon, dialogue and demand.

written 2005–2007

And Yet

I lay out syringe, alcohol pad, vial: a ritual
connecting me to junkies. Draw the testosterone,
and push needle deep through skin into muscle.

*And yet, I would have chosen hermit, storm–high river, heron flying
upstream.*

Open the windows, forsythia spills its dense yellow.

North on Baldwin Road, I walk my everyday walk.
Bottom of the hill, a dog barks, boy yells, "Hey mister.
Hey mister. Hey mister." We've traded names a dozen times.

Then "Hey retard. Retard. Retard."
Schoolyard to street corner: words
slung by the pocketful.

Crip skin marked,
white skin not.

Open the doors, daffodils rear their bright heads.

Cypionate suspended in cottonseed oil,
a shapeshifter's drug the color of pale sunlight:

Voice cracks.
Stubble glints.

Open the cellar. Soon, soon the maples will unfurl their green fists.

And yet, girl arrived first, bones set to the current.

In the mirror I wait,
the difference a simple ritual—
verb, skin, muscle, hormone.

Body begins.

Split the stone open, then the lilacs' deep purple.

In another time, at another place, I might have relied upon
insistent dreams; gods, goddesses, spirits all;
an herbalist stepping out back, nettle or ginseng.

Jaw squares.
Hips and ass slim.

> *And yet, had I been given a choice, they*
> *would have demanded clay or granite, salt*
> *water or fresh, as if the confluence could*
> *never be home.*

Open, palms stretched wide, apple orchard still bare boned.

But today I have Pfizer, Upjohn, Watson,
doctors saying yes, saying no, judging
the very stretch of skin over bone.

Crip skin,
white skin:
which stories
do I tell the best,
and which
rarely begin—
turn, flutter,
settle?

Open to the peepers, coyotes, faint crescent moon.

This drug I shoot in careful fractions:
I step into its exam rooms,
pay its bills, increase its profits.

Pecs bulk.
Skin roughens.

Body begins to settle.

Let them draw my blood, check
liver, kidney, cholesterol, hematocrit,
track the numbers, write the script.

Open, orchard soon to be enveloped in blossom.

Round the next bend, other boys want my name,
hand me theirs, ask as only 5–year–olds can,
"Why don't you talk so good?" I shrug, keep moving.

> And yet, here at the confluence, river and ocean
> collide—current rushing head long, waves pushing
> back—stones tumble, logs roll. Tell me: where
> in this hiss and froth might I lay myself down?

starting testosterone 2004
written 2004–2006

How to Talk to a New
Lover About Cerebral Palsy

Tell her: *Complete strangers*
have patted my head, kissed
my cheek, called me courageous.

Tell this story more than once, ask
her to hold you, rock you
against her body, breast to back,

her arms curving round, only
you flinch unchosen, right arm trembles.
Don't use the word *spastic*.

> In Europe after centuries
> of death by exposure
> and drowning,
> they banished us
> to the streets.

Let her feel the tension burn down your arms,
tremors jump. Take it slow: when she asks
about the difference between CP and MS,

refrain from handing her an encyclopedia.
If you leave, know that you will ache.
Resist the urge to ignore your body. Tell her:

They taunted me retard, monkey,
defect. *The words sank into my body.*
The rocks and fists left bruises.

Gimps and crips, caps
in hand, we still
wander the streets but now
the options abound: telethons,
nursing homes, welfare lines.

Try not to be ashamed as you flinch and tremble
under her warm hands. Think of the stories you haven't
told yet. Tension locks behind your shoulder blades.

Ask her what she thinks as your hands shake
along her body, sleep curled against her,
and remember to listen: she might surprise you.

everyday encounters
written 1992

Photographs

I.

Fingers splayed and reaching,
odd angle of wrist and grin—
facing pages, two women:
one plays in the tide, face tilted
to sun. I follow
her legs down to the feet
she doesn't have. Retreating
surf leaves sand
soft and loose against
her stumps.
              The other rolls
her head away from the camera,
long corridor in the background. She
holds hands with someone beyond
the frame, walls
the color of lichen.

II.

body against body
we tumble   roll   rise
arrive again   tongue to tooth   hand
balancing   small of back
sweet sweet skin   shining sweat
we think   coil and release   but soon
it will be   a thoughtless rhythm   breath
to muscle to ragged   breath

III.

You gain your entrance, call
the photos *inner grace*, nursing homes
and psych wards. Tell me:
did that woman in the corridor
invite your camera?

You unfold your tripod,
frame your pictures, press
the shutter. Every day someone
gawks, whispers, turns away,

and when you leave,
doors will lock behind you.
The woman laughing
in the surf,
she was out
on a day pass.

IV.

bodies tumble   roll
rise   *crazy   clumsy*   arriving
again   body against
body   *awkward*
ugly   each inviting
the next   tongue to tooth   sweet
sweet skin   *twisted*
deformed   a thoughtless
rhythm   *freak   monster*   breath to muscle
to ragged   breath   grace lives
tangled and strong

looking at photographs by Abraham Menashe 1992
written 1992, 2007

Battle Rock

I.

*We were landed at Port Orford on the morning of the 9th of June 1851.**

Driftwood lines the cliffs,
bone white and rough,
a jungle gym of logs.

> remember when
> surf at low tide
> could knock you over

June, 1851: nine white men
drew the port on their maps,
summer wind bellowing,

We found the Indians, who made their appearance when we first landed, to be somewhat friendly, manifesting a disposition to trade with us.

and still Main Street whistles,
creaks, fishermen tie
their boats tight.

---

* The italicized passages come from the personal letters of Captain J. M. Kirkpatrick, one of the white explorers who "founded" Port Orford, Oregon.

remember when you swung
long whips of bull kelp
overhead, round and round

*This did not last longer than the steamer lay at bay. As soon as
she left, the Indians grew saucy and ordered us off.*

Gulls circle all day,
beggars and outlaws waiting
for the fishing boats to return.

June, 1851: the Kwatami gathered
their weapons. Smallpox and alcohol
already littered the beaches.

*We took possession of a small island or rock. We had a four-
pounder cannon, which we brought from the steamer. This we
planted in front of our encampment.*

remember when you chased
waves barefoot down
to hubbards creek

High tide drums
the rocks, then recedes.

*In the morning the Indians began to gather on the beach in con-
siderable numbers. I noticed that they were better armed than
when we first landed.*

Green purple orange starfish
hold to crevices.

II.

Fourth of July in Port Orford:
the mounted posse leads the parade,
playground smelling of charcoal, beer,
barbecued salmon. I wander
the swarming town, ragged
and whitewashed, wait
through dinghy boat races,
sand castle contest, quilt raffle,
horse games, flags flap,
on every street corner.

Before dusk we settle
on the bluffs, air full of smoke
bombs. White boys dressed
as Indians leap around a bonfire.
I want to scuffle in the surf
with them half-naked, face
and chest painted red blue yellow.

Down the beach
white men dressed
as themselves climb
Battle Rock, drag
a cannon behind them,
rifles loaded.
They fire blanks, wait
for the boys to come
scrambling up the path.
I wheedle money
for one last cotton candy,
whistle and clap,

know that Mr. Peterson,
born-again preacher,
newspaper editor,
will declare victory,
lead a cheer.

And then it's dark,
fireworks spread across
the sky, bursts of color twirl
against stars, sound
of horns, surf, sizzle
of rockets lifting off.
I am convinced each burst
will land in my lap. Later
I follow my parents home,
half-asleep, confused
by cars, headlights,
streams of people.

III.

Savages, rogues, natives, redskins:
what did you call yourselves before
those nine white men arrived, sick
with goldrush fever?

You built cedar houses half underground.
Traded beads, shells, acorns. Measured
your plenty in gift giving. Burnt grass
as an offering to the salmon. This
is a half vision.

They then made a rush to pitch into camp among us, the chief
leading the way. The great crowd of them were within six feet
of the mouth of the cannon.

We climbed that rock again and again,
parents warning against poison oak.

Guns, felling axes, negotiated lies: you fought
desperate battles, learned the art of ambush and
blood.

I jerked up a firebrand and discharged the cannon among them,
killing some six or eight dead. The fight lasted about 15 min-
utes, when the Indians broke and ran.

Did you burn your dead,
let the tide carry their ashes away
like so many pieces of shell?
You joined the Takelmas and Latgawas,
waged a war that lasted many months.

They fled to the hills and rocks, and continued to shoot their
arrows at us for some time. There were a great many of them
wounded.

Now, a photograph,
black and white silhouette,
rock against ocean.

They rounded you up,
a long forced migration
north and east over the mountains,
another bitter trail.

During the afternoon, the chief came up the beach, and made
signs that he wanted to come into camp. He threw his arms
down on the sand,

The reservation at the end,
you began your lives again, middle
of sagebrush country:

*and made signs he wanted to take away the dead. This we let
him do.*

no ocean,
no salmon,
no rain, no
huckleberries
salal
Sitka spruce,

and every year
we dress ourselves
in mockery.

*battle of battle rock 1851, fourth of july celebration 1970s
written 1991*

TheTerrorist God

the one dressed in blue eyes
white skin who lives
not   in tree roots   fingertips
horse tails   he who swears
against sex   god of
witch burning   jew killing
consort of smallpox

let me talk to him   not
his popester   not his jesus
not his pedophiles   the big
man   the mean man   the sadist
in the sky   let me
bring him down

take a walk   sea
to shining sea   crack house
to uranium tailings   watch
a sunset   a moonrise   visit
a psych ward   lead him
quiet to the torture chambers
arrange meetings with
leonard peltier   angela
davis   césar chavéz   harriet
tubman   barbara deming
joseph beam   audre lorde
wilma mankiller   emma
goldman   leave the prisons
ringing dead and alive

there will be no
confession   no blood
and body   no penance   only

this pocketful of dirt
salt water and fresh
stones and stars

christian missionaries arrive in North America 1500s
written 1995

Escape

Father of mine, I have a myth I tell myself. Not memory. Not fiction. Just clues tied one to the next as I walk the North Shore, sit among skeletal birch, watch gulls nestle between waves.

You landed in Duluth at 21, first teaching job, first time away. Your father the gravedigger, your mother who tried to leave once and failed, your brother the bully. That dirt farm you called home. There could not be enough miles. You drove them wildly, carefully, deliriously numb.

a myth grasping at hope, love, the ways an imagined escape might turn real

You came here to the North Shore, fleeing ritual abuse. You must not have remembered any of it, body split from body. But as surely as I grew up with scar and aftershock, so did you before me. The gravedigger placed electrodes on your soft skin too, pulled you to the fire to watch cats burn down to their bones.

memory becomes a gift, a trial, an open door

In Duluth I you started to drink—cheap red wine, maybe whiskey or scotch on bad nights. Every morning before school you walked the Lake, five, six, seven miles; long flat horizon reassuring you.

if only this myth had been true

Every afternoon you went to Mass. But the blood and body offered by those men in black robes and white collars were not the real thing, and you hungered. You spent many a night barely containing

the frenzy in your body, wanting with every cell to
return to the gravedigger, wait your turn for the
blood, knives, children spread wide. In this myth you
are just a man trying to escape.

    i know well how the nighttime terrors arrive—
whirlwind, avalanche, rip tide

    After Duluth, you joined the army, married my
mother, moved to Pittsburgh, earned a Master's
degree. But at some moment, you started going back.
I know this because you took me to visit the
gravedigger every summer, because you found a man
just like him in your new home, halfway across the
country from the dirt farm.

    i too drove those miles numb, delirious,
careful

    Sky and lake surly gray, imagination becomes
a room, walls painted white, broad oak floor. I duck
inside to stand at the window, wind rising. I turn to
the things I can touch. Palm to bark. Palm to water.
Palm to mud.

    your escape waited one generation for me

dealing with ritual abuse 1992–2002
written 1996, 2007

Interlude VI: Launch

Tell it, talk it, translate it across divides of power, but let's not forget our own communities: passing transsexual folks who won't be seen with genderqueer folk and genderqueers who scorn the choice to transition. Parapalegics who pity quadrapalegics and quads who use the words retard and crazy in derision. Poor people who hate working-class people and working-class people who insist poor people are lazy moochers. People who use the same words to name their deepest selves and assume commonality, only to find themselves caught in disagreement.

Every time I watch tension flare along one of these fault lines, I want to say: tell a story, not one but two. Let them both repeat and contradict each other. Speak even as you don't know what will be heard. Listen even if you don't understand all the words.

*Create the space to tell it—*I used to walk down to the hayfields and sheep pastures, soaking sun, sky, cloud, whirr of grasshopper, into me even before I stood, wind against back, and launched my kite into its tug, soar, dance. The space to be heard and recognized. *The space to make it bigger than any single story.*

The marrow is a shadblow tree, a tangle, a
confluence.

written 2005-2007

Stone

Floating down a glacier-carved river, water roiling around boulders big as boxcars, banks lined with rock, worn smooth, warmed to the sun, I tell friends, "In my next life, I want to be a stone, a rock face sloped into the current, a boulder at the lip." We all laugh. I sift sand and gravel through my fingers.

\ \ \ \ \

Some nights when my father and his buddies tied me down, took fire to my skin, nights when they locked me in a cage or hung me from a rafter, my body shattered. But other nights—hour heaped upon hour, muscle contracting against contraction—turned my body to stone. I'd reach deep into the quiet. Settle beneath breath, pain, sound, beneath bone and blood.

Stone untouched and untouchable. But inside lies another stone called pain. It has put me to bed at night, woken me up in the morning, knocked me to the ground. Pain is my stone body softening, contradictory but true. And inside pain lives yet another stone, geode cracked to amethyst.

Body of stone: let me respectfully leave you behind. And as for pain, the knots and splinters, ruptures and breaks, I can only hope one day I'll be done with you. But the geode broken open to its hollow-skinned center, mountain range of crystal—pink, lavender, midnight purple—giving way but not yielding its strength: in this stone I want to make home.

Dream: I take the weight of your breasts into both hands, watch your eyes close. We kiss deep, then deeper as dusk rises round us. Tongue and tooth, skin and muscle, I cover your body with mine, rock against your hips, riding wide open into you. And when you reach toward me, I no longer flinch but accept only the briefest of touch, winding my hands through your hair.

\\\\\

In my next life, let me cradle into earth, giving way to wind, rain, ice, gravity, a boulder at the lip.

returning to my body 1996–2000
written 1998, 2007

In the Woodshop

Cradle this box in your palm,
walnut and oak sanded
to silky line of sternum,
dark wood inlaid into light,
latch waits for your finger
to find its soft indent—peonies
on the brink of blossom. Lid tumbles
til the box lies flat, skin of wood
against skin of hand: muscle releases
bone, corn rocks crib, heron tiptoes
toward salmon, and when
those four walls fold up again,
bevel nestled into bevel, what
will they contain: stone soft as clay,
bone fiercely hollow?

bodywork 1994–2002
written 1996

Left with the Ocean

Falling asleep, your breath falling
deeper, I curve my body around yours:

fog still thick down
to Sixes River, barefoot

I climb the headland
to lie among wild

strawberries, spread the grass
and pick them sweet in the sun.

Wind blows beach ragged
on the north side, surf high

against rock, curve of cape
protects the south side, leaves

a long flat beach,
waves so steady until

my breath
settles into yours. I fall asleep.

relationship 1987
written 1987, 2007

Stars

I drift,
am pulled,
arrive
without a map.
Stars fall, a steady
mist, they talk
slow intimate
detail, teach me
to leap, space
between sun
and fog.
We celebrate
winter's
first freshet.

finding community 1984–1990
written 1992

Two Waters

for Samuel Benjamin

This place where two waters meet,
we lay our bodies down,
sky folding over us. Stories fall like rain,
spar trees weathered to bone.

We lay our bodies down,
bones beginning to breathe,
spar trees weathered to bone,
words shimmering into kisses.

Bones begin to breathe,
skin drips sweat, glinting,
words shimmer to kisses
layered in cinnamon and salt,

skin dripping sweat, glints.
Tell me a dream, and I'll tell you a vision
in cinnamon and salt, newly turned dirt:
a child turning to river, to wind, to boulder.

Tell me a dream, and I'll tell you a vision,
years measured in miles and miles in grief.
A child turning to river, to wind, to boulder:
he learned to walk a knotted road.

Years measured in miles and miles
spun to smoke, to mist, to motes of sun.
He learned to walk a knotted road,
and in its place we wake, grief

spun to smoke, to mist, to motes of sun,
my hands playing their unsteady beat,
tremor to skin, we wake
the warm hollow center,

hands dance that unsteady beat,
this place where two waters meet,
the center waits warm and hollow,
sky folded over, stories falling like rain.

relationship 2000–present
written 2001

About the Author

White, disabled, and genderqueer, Eli Clare has a B.A. in Women's Studies, a M.F.A. in Creative Writing, and most importantly a penchant for rabble-rousing. Among other pursuits, he has walked across the United States for peace, coordinated a rape prevention program, and helped organize the first ever Queerness and Disability Conference. He has spoken all over the United States at conferences, community events, and colleges about disability, queer identities, and social justice. Eli is the author of *Exile and Pride: Disability, Queerness, and Liberation* (South End Press, 1999) and has been published in many periodicals and anthologies. He lives in Vermont and works at the University of Vermont's LGBTQA Services.

Made in the USA
Las Vegas, NV
31 October 2022

58512238R00070